SECOND EDITION

# EXPLORE
# Geography Picture
# Dictionary

Ballard & Tighe

Brea, California

## AUTHORS

**Roberta Stathis**, Ph.D., is an educator, writer, and editor. She received a bachelor of arts degree with honors in anthropology and social sciences and a master of arts degree in education from California State University, San Bernardino. She earned a Ph.D. in education from the Claremont Graduate University. Stathis is the author of *Explore World History*.

**Leila A. Langston**, B.A., is a graduate of Occidental College, California. She has extensive teaching experience and also has served as a learning specialist and ESL program coordinator. Langston is the author of *Carousel of IDEAS*, *Explore the Ancient World*, and *Explore the United States*, and co-author of *IDEAS for Literature* and *Explore America*.

**Carin Dewhirst**, M.Ed., is a graduate of Occidental College, California and Columbia University, New York. She has written eight children's books, including adaptions of *Peter and the Wolf* and *The Nutcracker*, as well as *My Tricks and Treats*, *Lullabies and Bedtime Stories*, and *Strike Up the Orchestra!: A Guide to Classical Music for Children*. She is a co-author of *Explore America* and contributor to *Explore the Ancient World*.

## GENERAL GEOGRAPHY EDITOR

**Mark P. Kumler** is an associate professor of geography at California State University, San Bernardino. He has fond memories of drawing maps of faraway places in school. He studied geography at Dartmouth College, Michigan State University, and the University of California at Santa Barbara, and he has traveled extensively throughout Europe, New Zealand, and North America. He enjoys teaching geography to his children with maps, globes, and books like this.

## REVIEWERS

The authors and publisher express grateful appreciation to the teachers and other educators who carefully reviewed the *Explore Geography Picture Dictionary* and provided helpful comments and suggestions:

Suzanne M. Hidalgo, San Bernardino City Unified School District, Highland, California
Norma Inabinette, Springville, California
Erik B. Johansen, Oxnard Union High School District, Oxnard, California
Martha J. Kemp, Phoenix Union High School District, Glendale, Arizona
Conrad Nicoll, California State University, Fullerton, California
Paul Watlington, Falls Church High School District, Falls Church, Virginia

## PHOTO & ILLUSTRATION CREDITS

(t=top, b=bottom, c=center)

Page: 5, (b) Paul Helmle; 6, (c) Sabrina Lammé; 7, (c) Emmy Rhee (b) Courtesy of Grand Canyon Explorer, www.kaibab.org; 8, (t) Tom Sullivan, www.geocities.com/Paris/4118/index.html (b) Keith Neely; 14, (c) Emmy Rhee; 15, (t) Emmy Rhee; 16, (b) Heera Kang; 17, (b) Donald Schwert, Department of Geosciences, North Dakota State University; 18, (t) Keith Neely (c) Michelle Chew (b) Marvin J. Malecha, FAIA; 19, (t) Emmy Rhee (b) Sabrina Lammé; 20, (t) Aileen Buckley; 21, (b) Keith Neely; 24, (t) Leilani Trollinger; 25, (t) Emmy Rhee; 27, (b) Patricia P. Miller; 28, (b) Elaine Elwell; 29, (c) Library of Congress; 31, (t) Emmy Rhee; 32, (c) Dover Publications; 33, (b) Keith Neely; 36, (t) Emmy Rhee (b) Courtesy of Grand Canyon Explorer, www.kaibab.org; 39, (t) Erik Jones, Esq. (b) Emmy Rhee; 40, (b) Visuals Unlimited, Inc.; 42, (t) John Oswalt, www.jao.com; 43, (b) Emmy Rhee; 45, (c) Jim De Forge; 46, (t) Dorothy Roberts; 47, (t) Emmy Rhee (c) Twila Bing (b) Edith Leiby; 48, (c) Emmy Rhee (b) Sabrina Lammé; 49, (t) Emmy Rhee; 50, (t) Keith Neely

Every effort has been made to trace the copyright holders, and we apologize in advance for any omissions. We would be pleased to insert the appropriate acknowledgment in any subsequent edition of this book.

### An IDEA® Content Resource from Ballard & Tighe

Managing Editor: Laurie Regan
Editorial Project Manager: Allison Mangrum (second edition), Heera Kang (first edition)
Program Consultants: David Brisco, Patrice Gotsch, Jill Kinkade, Leonor Morris
Editorial Assistant: Kristin Belsher
Art Director: Kathy Spear
Desktop Publishing Coordinator: Kathleen Styffe
Graphic Designer: Charles W. Shaffer, III

2005 Printing
ISBN 1-55501-549-2    Catalog #2-670

Brea, California • (800) 321-4332 • www.ballard-tighe.com

# Contents

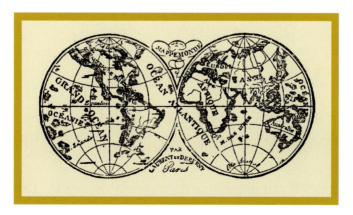

# Introduction

## Can You Pronounce *Archipelago*?

Can you name the tallest mountain in the world? Do you know what a gazetteer is? Do you know why the Dead Sea is "dead"? The *Explore Geography Picture Dictionary* answers all of these questions and more! Look inside and you will find places, names, facts, and figures that will help you understand the world. And the more you know, the more you will realize that the earth is an amazing place.

All of the information in the *Explore Geography Picture Dictionary* is easy to find and easy to understand. Everything is arranged in alphabetical order. For example, *archipelago* is a snap to find: it's between *aqueduct* and *atlas*.

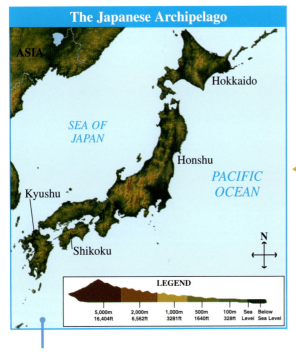

The **pronunciation guide** is right after the word. This is a special spelling that shows you how to say the word. The hyphens (-) tell where the word is divided into syllables or units of sound. The syllable in all capital letters, "PEL" in this case, is the part of the word to stress.

**archipelago**: (ahr-kuh-PEL-uh-goh) *n.* A large group of islands. The Japanese archipelago includes four main islands and more than 4,000 smaller islands.

The **definition** tells what the word means. If one of the words in the definition is printed in red (such as islands here), then there is an entry in this dictionary for that word as well. Sometimes there are examples in parentheses after the letters "e.g." This abbreviation ("e.g.") comes from two Latin words, *exempli gratia*, that mean "for example."

For more information, read the sentence after the definition. **Reading a word in a sentence** can help you understand its meaning.

A **colorful map, photograph, or drawing** shows you a picture of each geographical term. For example, this map shows a picture of an archipelago.

## Who Said, "No Man Is an Island"?

You'll find the answer in one of the many **Voices in Geography** sections. These quotations relate to geography and are from famous people. By the way, John Donne wrote, "No man is an island" about 400 years ago.

Want more facts? The **Fun Facts** tell you interesting things about the world. Did you know that Greenland is the largest island in the world?

The *Explore Geography Picture Dictionary* is designed to help you learn about our amazing world.

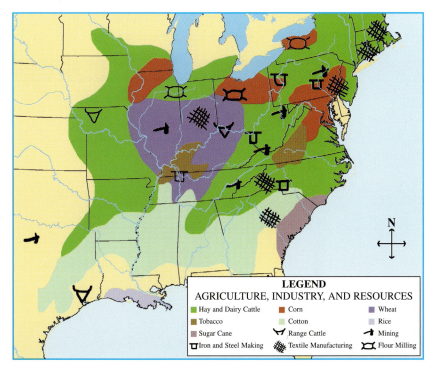

LEGEND
AGRICULTURE, INDUSTRY, AND RESOURCES

| | | |
|---|---|---|
| 🟩 Hay and Dairy Cattle | 🟥 Corn | 🟪 Wheat |
| 🟫 Tobacco | 🟩 Cotton | Rice |
| Sugar Cane | Range Cattle | Mining |
| Iron and Steel Making | Textile Manufacturing | Flour Milling |

**agriculture, industry, and resources map**: (AG-ri-kuhl-chur, IN-duhs-tree, and REE-sohr-sez MAP) *n.* A map that shows the crops, industries, and natural resources of an area. This agriculture, industry, and resources map shows four major areas where people make steel and iron.

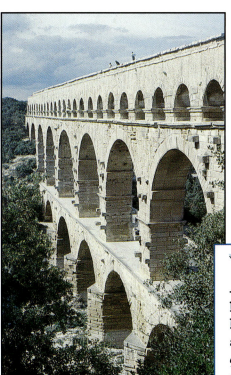

**aqueduct**: (AK-wuh-dukt) *n.* A bridge or other structure that helps move water in a certain direction. This aqueduct was built more than 1,000 years ago by the ancient Romans. See IRRIGATION SYSTEMS.

  FUN FACTS

Romans were the first people to build aqueducts. By A.D. 97, aqueducts brought 85 million gallons of water into Rome every day. That's enough water to fill 850 large swimming pools every day.

"No man is an island."

—John Donne, 1624

**archipelago**: (ahr-kuh-PEL-uh-goh) *n.* A large group of islands. The Japanese archipelago includes four main islands and more than 4,000 smaller islands.

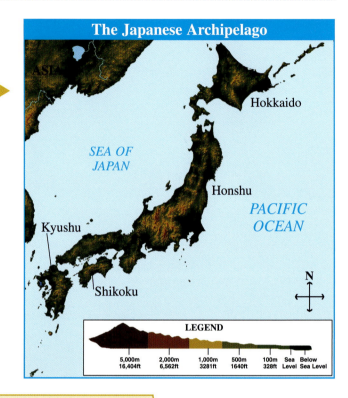

### The Japanese Archipelago

ASIA

Hokkaido

SEA OF JAPAN

Honshu

PACIFIC OCEAN

Kyushu

Shikoku

N

**LEGEND**

| 5,000m 16,404ft | 2,000m 6,562ft | 1,000m 3281ft | 500m 1640ft | 100m 328ft | Sea Level | Below Sea Level |

  **FUN FACTS**

Abraham Cresques created the Catalan Atlas in the late 1300s as a gift for the king of France. This atlas described the riches of Africa where gold "grew like carrots."

**atlas**: (AT-lus) *n.* A book that contains maps and charts. You can use an atlas to find maps of the world.

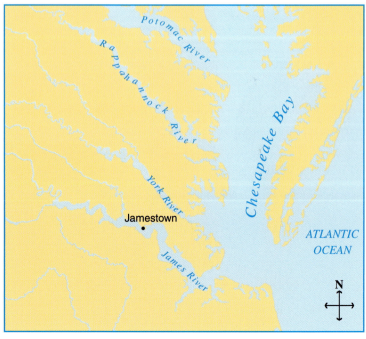

Potomac River

Rappahannock River

Chesapeake Bay

York River

Jamestown

ATLANTIC OCEAN

James River

N

**bay**: (bay) *n.* A part of the ocean going into the land. As this map shows, many rivers flow into Chesapeake Bay.

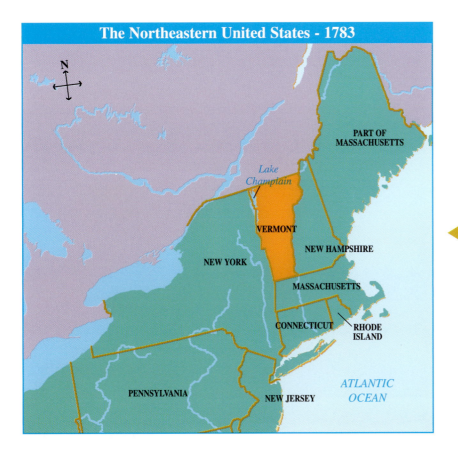

## The Northeastern United States - 1783

N

PART OF
MASSACHUSETTS

*Lake Champlain*

VERMONT

NEW HAMPSHIRE

NEW YORK

MASSACHUSETTS

CONNECTICUT    RHODE
ISLAND

PENNSYLVANIA

NEW JERSEY

*ATLANTIC OCEAN*

**boundary**: (BOWN-duh-ree) *n.* A line marking the border between two areas. This map of the United States in 1783 shows that Lake Champlain forms part of Vermont's western boundary.

**canal**: (kuh-NAL) *n.* A ditch or other waterway dug into the ground to carry the flow of water. Farmers sometimes use canals to bring water to their fields. See IRRIGATION SYSTEMS.

canal

**canyon**: (KAN-yun) *n.* A deep, narrow valley. You can see a river at the bottom of this canyon.

**cape**: (kayp) *n.* A narrow piece of land that sticks out into a sea or other body of water; similar to a peninsula, only smaller. Prince Henry of Portugal studied navigation at Cape St. Vincent.

**cataract**: (KAT-uh-rakt) *n.* A large waterfall or steep rapids. The cataracts of the Nile River are steep rapids.

 **FUN FACTS**

The second cataract of the Nile River is now under the waters of Lake Nassar. Lake Nassar was created when the Aswan High Dam was built in 1970.

## HOW A CAVE IS MADE

1. *Water dissolves limestone. It makes an underground cave.*

2. *The water level drops, leaving the cave dry.*

3. *Rocks fall and cover the mouth of the cave.*

**cave**: (kayv) *n.* An opening in a hillside. The drawing (left) shows how a cave is made. The picture (below) shows a photograph of a cave.

**channel**: (CHAN-ul) *n.* A wide passage of water joining two larger bodies of water. The waterway that separates Great Britain and the European mainland is called the English Channel. See STRAIT.

NORTH SEA

IRELAND

GREAT BRITAIN

ATLANTIC OCEAN

English Channel

EUROPE

N

**city**: (SIT-ee) *n.* A place where people live that is larger and has more people than a town or village. A city has many buildings and roads.

9

"Geography is both science and art."

—H.C. Darby, 1962

**cliff**: (klif) *n.* A high, steep rock. This photograph shows a very steep cliff.

**climate**: (KLIY-mut) *n.* The long-term, average weather conditions. The map below shows three major types of climate—tropical (hot), temperate (mild), and polar (very cold).

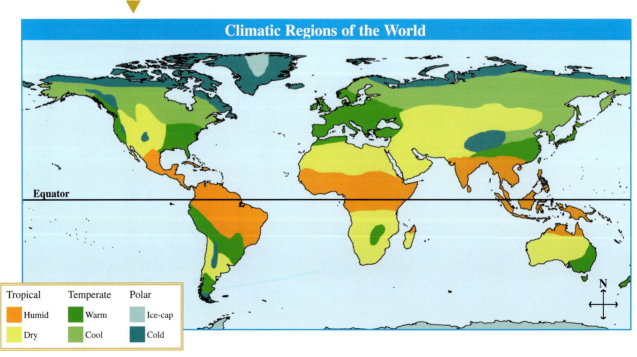

**Climatic Regions of the World**

Equator

| Tropical | Temperate | Polar |
|---|---|---|
| Humid | Warm | Ice-cap |
| Dry | Cool | Cold |

N

**Northwest Coast of North America**

N

TLINGIT

HAIDA — TSIMSHIAN

BELLA COOLA
KWAKIUTL

NOOTKA

QUILEUTE
QUINAULT — Canada
CHINOOK
TILLAMOOK — Washington

KLIKITAT

Oregon

California

**coast**: (kohst) *n.* The land along the water. Many American Indian tribes settled along the Northwest Coast of North America.

**commercial harbor**: (kuh-MUR-shul HAHR-bur) *n.* A harbor with docks and other facilities so that ships can load and unload their cargo. This picture shows a busy commercial harbor in Hawaii.

**compass rose**: (KUHM-pus ROHZ) *n.* A symbol on a map that shows directions such as north, south, east, and west. Most maps include a compass rose. It can be very simple or very elaborate.

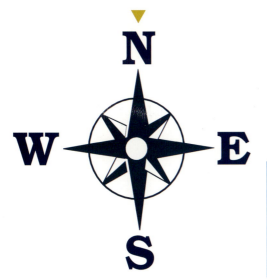

 **FUN FACTS**

People have used the compass rose symbol since the 1300s. Its name comes from the similarity of the compass points to the petals of a rose.

11

## ⊕ *Voices in Geography* ⊕

"Journey over all the universe in a map without the expense and fatigue of traveling …"

—Miguel de Cervantes (1547-1616)

**continent**: (KAHN-tuh-nent) *n.* One of the seven major landmasses of the earth— Africa, Antarctica, Asia, Australia, Europe, North America, and South America. Asia is the largest continent on earth.

**Continental Divide**: (KAHN-tuh-nent-ul duh-VIYD) *n.* The ridge of the Rocky Mountains that separates rivers flowing toward the east from those flowing toward the west. All the rivers to the west of the Continental Divide flow toward the Pacific Ocean. All the rivers to the east flow toward the Atlantic Ocean.

**dam**: (dam) *n.* Something (a barrier) built across a waterway to control the flow or raise the level of water. People build dams for many reasons, including to prevent flooding. See IRRIGATION SYSTEMS.

**degree**: (duh-GREE) *n.* A unit of measurement used to describe latitude or longitude. The symbol is a raised circle, so 45° is "forty-five degrees." Sailors keep track of their location by knowing their degree of latitude and longitude. See EQUATOR and PRIME MERIDIAN. (Units of degrees are used to describe other measurements including temperature.)

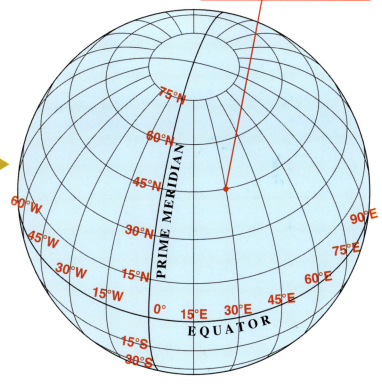

point located at 45°N, 30°E

**delta**: (DEL-tuh) *n.* A deposit of sand and soil at the mouth of some rivers. A delta is usually shaped like a triangle. The delta of the Nile River has rich and fertile soil.

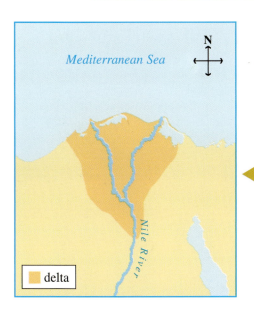

Mediterranean Sea

N

Nile River

delta

**demographic change**: (dem-uh-GRAF-ik CHAYNJ) *n.* A change in the size, distribution (e.g., where people live), or composition (e.g., age, gender, or ethnicity) of a population. This chart shows a large demographic change. In the 50-year period between 1870 and 1920, many Americans moved to urban areas.

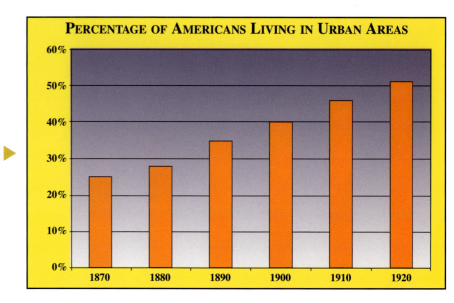

**PERCENTAGE OF AMERICANS LIVING IN URBAN AREAS**

**depth**: (depth) *n.* The distance from sea level to the bottom of an ocean, sea, lake, or other body of water. Scientists measure the depth of oceans with scientific instruments.

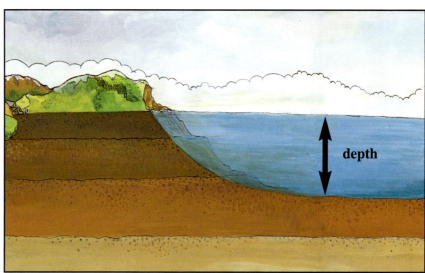

depth

**desert**: (DEZ-urt) *n.* A region of the earth that gets very little rainfall (fewer than 10 inches per year). The Sahara desert has no trees and very little plant or animal life.

 **FUN FACTS**

The Sahara desert is the largest desert in the world.

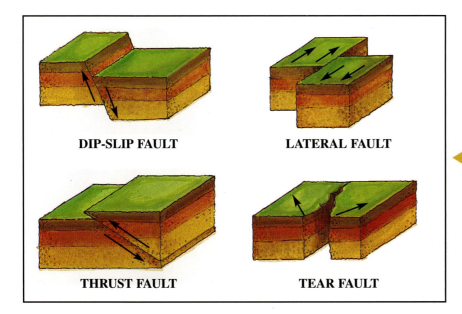

**DIP-SLIP FAULT**

**LATERAL FAULT**

**THRUST FAULT**

**TEAR FAULT**

**earthquake**: (URTH-kwayk) *n.* A movement in the earth's surface caused by shifting tectonic plates or volcanic activity. This drawing shows four different kinds of faults. When the earth's surface moves along a fault, it causes an earthquake.

22,834 feet

**elevation**: (el-uh-VAY-shun) *n.* A word that describes the height of mountains and other natural features; elevation is usually measured in feet or meters using sea level (which is 0 elevation) as the starting point. The Andes Mountains reach elevations of more than 22,000 feet.

 **FUN FACTS**

The Andes in South America are the second tallest mountains in the world. Did you know that potatoes can grow on the Andes at higher than 10,000 feet?

15

**environmental pollution**: (en-VIY-ruhn-ment-ul puh-LOO-shun) *n.* Contamination of the earth's water, air, or soil. These factories put chemicals into the air, causing environmental pollution.

**NORTHERN HEMISPHERE**

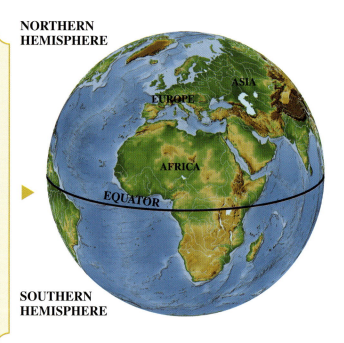

EUROPE

ASIA

AFRICA

EQUATOR

**equator**: (i-KWAY-tur) *n.* An imaginary line that goes around the middle of the earth. The area north of the equator is in the Northern Hemisphere and the area south of the equator is in the Southern Hemisphere. The latitude of the equator is 0°. Because the equator runs through the middle of Africa, part of the African continent is in the Northern Hemisphere and part is in the Southern Hemisphere.

**SOUTHERN HEMISPHERE**

**erosion**: (ee-ROH-zhun) *n.* The wearing away of soil material from the earth's surface. Erosion can be a serious problem for farmers.

# 🌐 *Voices in Geography* 🌐

"Geography will aim to make clear the relationships existing between natural environments and the distribution and activities of man."

—Harland H. Barrows, 1923

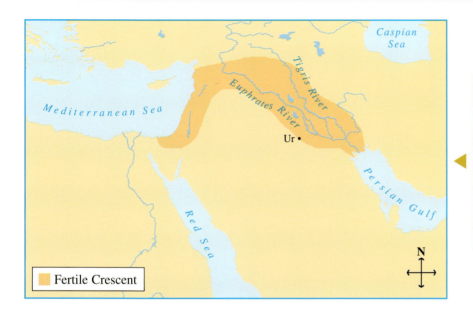

**Fertile Crescent**: (FURT-ul KRES-ent) *n.* A region of rich, fertile soil that stretches from the Mediterranean Sea, between the Tigris and Euphrates rivers, to the Persian Gulf. Many ancient civilizations began in the Fertile Crescent.

**flood plain**: (FLUHD PLAYN) *n.* A flat area of land that is covered by water when the rivers or streams in the area overflow. Living on a flood plain can be dangerous if the nearby rivers overflow.

**foothill**: (FUT-hil) *n.*  A low hill at the bottom of a mountain.  The small hills at the bottom of these tall mountains are called foothills.  See PIEDMONT.

**forest**: (FOHR-ist) *n.*  A large area of land covered with trees and thick brush.  During the Middle Ages, people of Europe cut down many forests so they could plant crops on the land.

**frontier**: (fruhn-TEER) *n.*  The part of a country that borders another country or an undeveloped region.  The Chinese built the Great Wall to protect their frontier from invaders.

**gap**: (gap) *n.*  A steep, narrow pass through a hill or mountain.  A gap is made by wind or water.  See MOUNTAIN PASS and RAVINE.

gap

**gazetteer**: (gaz-uh-TEER) *n.* A geographical dictionary that includes brief descriptions about places.  You can look in a gazetteer to find information about the place where you live.

 FUN FACTS

The first gazetteer was published in 1693 and was called "The Newsman's Interpreter: Being a Geographical Index."

**geographer**: (jee-AHG-ruh-fur) *n.* A person who studies geography. People who want to be geographers go to college to learn about the earth and its features. This photograph shows geographers using a tool to collect information.

**geography**: (jee-AHG-ruh-fee) *n.* The study of the earth and its features. Geography also includes the study of how people interact with their environment. This chart shows five themes of geography—place, location, people and environment, movement, and regions.

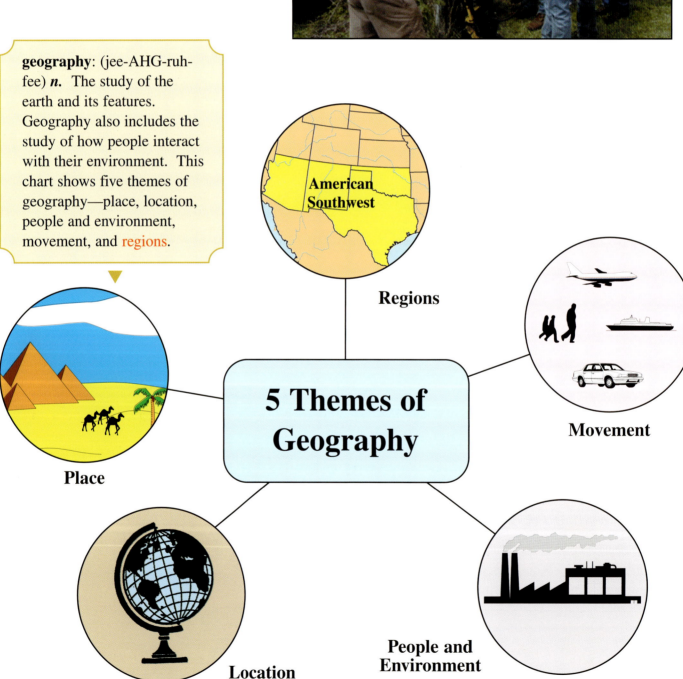

American Southwest

Regions

Movement

# 5 Themes of Geography

Place

Location

People and Environment

**glacier**: (GLAY-shur) *n.* A large mass of ice and snow that forms faster than the snow can melt. Sometimes people think of glaciers as rivers of ice. This glacier is in Alaska. There are more than 100,000 glaciers in Alaska.

 **FUN FACTS**

If you visit the New York Public Library, you can see one of the earliest globes. It was made in 1503. This globe even includes America because Columbus had just made his historic trip there.

**globe**: (glohb) *n.* A sphere (ball) that is a tiny model of the earth; it shows all the earth's land and water. A globe has many advantages over a flat map.

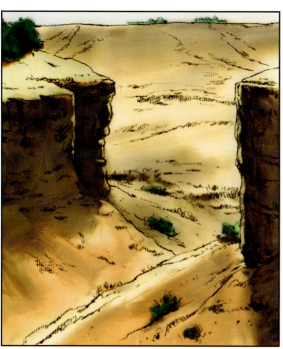

**gorge**: (gohrj) *n.* A deep, narrow pass with steep sides. Archaeologists found fossil bones in Olduvai Gorge in Africa.

**Great Lakes**: (GRAYT LAYKS) *n.* The five lakes—Huron, Ontario, Michigan, Erie, and Superior—located on either side of the U.S. and Canadian border. The Great Lakes are the largest group of freshwater lakes in the world.

**gulf**: (guhlf) *n.* A large area of sea or ocean partly enclosed by land. The city of Venice is located on the Gulf of Venice.

**harbor**: (HAHR-bur) *n.* A sheltered part of a body of water that is a safe place for ships. Plymouth Harbor looks small compared to the Atlantic Ocean, but it can hold many large ships. See COMMERCIAL HARBOR and PORT.

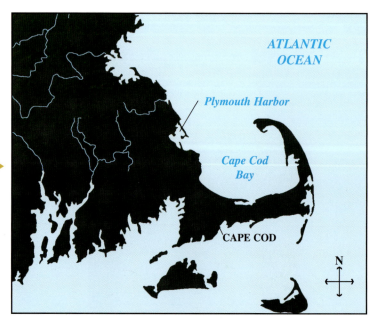

# 🌍 *Voices in Geography* 🌍

"I am not born for one corner; the whole world is my native land."

—Lucius Annaeus Seneca the Younger (4 B.C.–A.D. 65)

**hemisphere**: (HEM-i-sfeer) *n.* One half of the world—commonly used to refer to the northern or southern halves when divided by the equator, or the eastern or western halves when divided by the prime meridian. Africa is located in all four hemispheres.

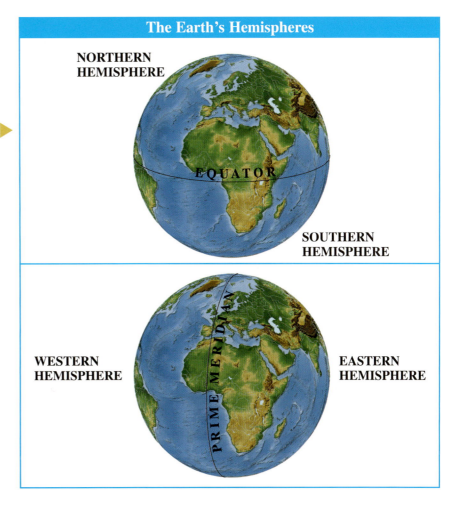

**The Earth's Hemispheres**

NORTHERN HEMISPHERE

EQUATOR

SOUTHERN HEMISPHERE

WESTERN HEMISPHERE

PRIME MERIDIAN

EASTERN HEMISPHERE

**hill**: (hil) *n.* Land that is higher than the ground around it. A hill is like a mountain, only smaller. See FOOTHILL and PIEDMONT.

23

# 🌍 *Voices in Geography* 🌍

"… [The] study of geography forces one to consider the whole earth, it forces comparisons between countries, and people, and cultures."

—*Christian Science Monitor*, 1919

**inlet**: (IN-let) *n.* A narrow stream of water that goes inland from an ocean, river, or lake. Native Americans in the Pacific Northwest traveled in canoes over inlets.

**international date line**: (in-tuhr-NASH-uhn-ul DAYT liyn) *n.* An imaginary line that begins at the North Pole and then goes through the Pacific Ocean to the South Pole. By international agreement, the calendar date is one day earlier in the area to the east of the international date line.

  **FUN FACTS**

All the world has agreed that the international date line is where travelers change dates. When we travel eastward, we subtract a day. When we travel westward, we add a day.

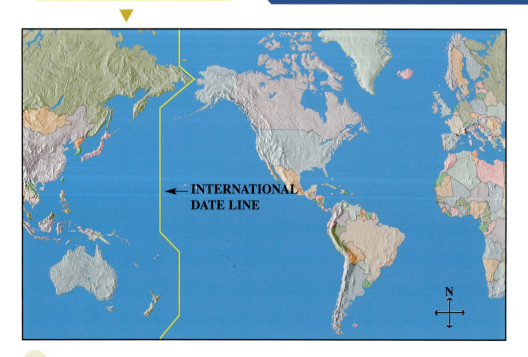

← INTERNATIONAL DATE LINE

**irrigation systems**: (ir-i-GAY-shun SIS-tumz) *n.* Methods to supply land with water, including dams, canals, and aqueducts. Farmers use irrigation systems to bring water to their fields.

**island**: (IY-lund) *n.* A piece of land surrounded completely by water. Some islands are called "continental islands" because they are pieces of a continent that have been separated from the mainland (e.g., Great Britain is a continental island). Some islands are called "oceanic islands" because they were formed by volcanoes on the ocean floor (e.g., the Hawaiian Islands are oceanic islands). This map shows one large island and several smaller ones. See ISLE and ARCHIPELAGO.

  FUN FACTS

In geography, the main difference between an island and a continent is size. But there is a big difference in size! The largest island is Greenland. But the largest continent, Asia, is 22 times larger than Greenland. In fact, Asia includes a third of the entire world's land area!

*Voices in Geography*

"Those who contemplate the beauty of the earth find reserves of strength that will endure as long as life lasts."

—Rachel Louise Carson (1907-1964)

**Great Britain**

**isle**: (iyl) *n.* A small island; a piece of land surrounded completely by water. There are many isles along the coast of Great Britain. See ARCHIPELAGO.

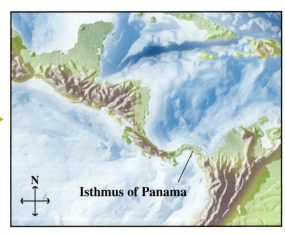

**isthmus**: (IS-mus) *n.* A narrow strip of land that connects two larger pieces of land. The United States built a canal across the Isthmus of Panama.

**Isthmus of Panama**

**lake**: (layk) *n.* A body of water that has land all around it. People settle near lakes because of the water, which supports plant and animal life.

# 🌐 *Voices in Geography* 🌐

"The kingdom [of Mali in Africa] is square in shape, being four months [of travel] in length and at least that much in breadth."

—Ibn Battuta, 1354

**land bridge**: (LAND BRIJ) *n.*
A piece of land that connects two pieces of land. During the ice ages, the water level in the oceans dropped to expose land and this made land bridges. Experts think the earliest people in North America came across a land bridge from Asia during the ice ages. This land bridge is now covered with water and is called the Bering Strait.

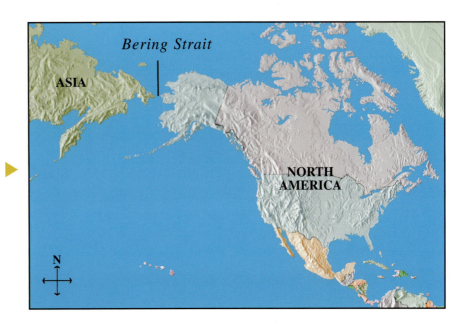

**landmark**: (LAND-mahrk) *n.*
A large, natural feature (such as a mountain) or cultural feature (such as a building). Landmarks can help people locate places. The Great Sphinx serves as a landmark for travelers in Egypt.

**landmass**: (LAND-mas) *n.*
A very large area of land, especially a continent. The continent of Africa is a huge landmass.

AFRICA

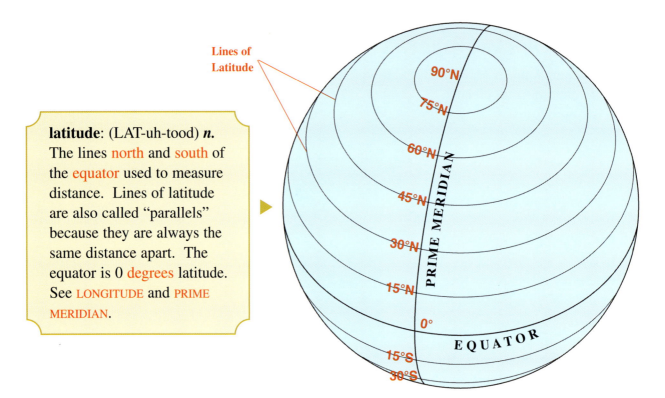

**Lines of Latitude**

**latitude**: (LAT-uh-tood) *n.* The lines north and south of the equator used to measure distance. Lines of latitude are also called "parallels" because they are always the same distance apart. The equator is 0 degrees latitude. See LONGITUDE and PRIME MERIDIAN.

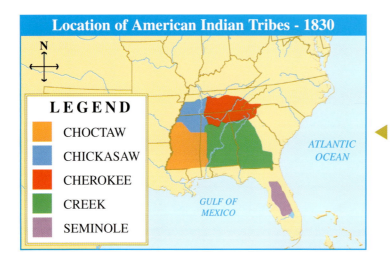

**Location of American Indian Tribes - 1830**

N

**LEGEND**

CHOCTAW
CHICKASAW
CHEROKEE
CREEK
SEMINOLE

ATLANTIC OCEAN

GULF OF MEXICO

**legend**: (LEJ-und) *n.* The words or symbols that explain how information is displayed on a map. A legend often is shown in a box on the map. Sometimes a legend is called a "key." Using the legend on this map, you can see the location of various American Indian tribes in 1830.

**loess highlands**: (LOH-es HIY-lundz) *n.* A high area above the North China Plain covered by deep layers of windblown yellow soil called loess. The Yellow River carries soil from the loess highlands to China's valleys and plains.

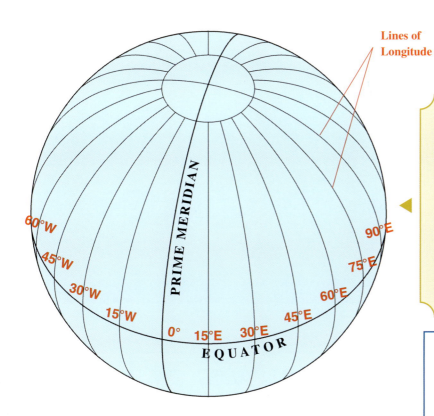

Lines of Longitude

**longitude**: (LAHN-juh-tood) **n.** The lines east and west of the prime meridian used to measure distance. Lines of longitude are also called meridians. Longitude is measured in degrees. The prime meridian is 0° longitude. See LATITUDE and PRIME MERIDIAN.

 **FUN FACTS**

The Babylonians made the first known map of the world. About 900 B.C., they carved the tiny map into wet clay and dried it in the sun. The map is only about the size of a playing card.

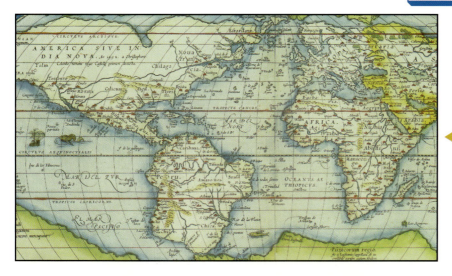

**map**: (map) **n.** A picture or drawing of a region of the earth or the planets. This is a map of the world made in 1570. See AGRICULTURE, INDUSTRY, AND RESOURCES MAP, PHYSICAL MAP, POLITICAL MAP, POPULATION MAP, RELIEF MAP, SPECIAL PURPOSE MAP, STREET MAP, TOPOGRAPHIC MAP, and VEGETATION MAP.

**marsh**: (mahrsh) **n.** An area of low, wet land; a bog or swamp. A marsh is not a good place to grow crops.

**mesa**: (MAY-suh) *n.* A small area of high, flat land. Some American Indians settled on mesas in the Southwest region of North America. See PLATEAU.

**mountain**: (MOWN-tun) *n.* A very high, natural elevation of the earth's surface with steep sides; a very high hill. Early European settlers in America crossed mountains as they moved westward.

 **FUN FACTS**

Mt. Everest is the tallest point on earth. It is part of the Himalaya Mountains in Asia. Mt. Everest is about 5½ miles above sea level.

"Mountains are earth's undecaying monuments."

—Nathaniel Hawthorne, 1868

**mountain pass**: (MOWN-tun pas) *n.* A gap (space) between mountains. Travelers are happy to find a mountain pass because it makes travel through tall mountains much faster. See GAP.

**mountain range**: (MOWN-tun raynj) *n.* A group of mountains forming a line. Mountain ranges affect the weather. Tall mountains catch winds and this results in rain.

"In our every deliberation, we must consider the impact of our decisions on the next seven generations."
—From the Great Law of the Iroquois Confederacy, c. 1450

**natural boundary**: (NACH-uhr-ul BOWN-duh-ree) **n.** Something natural (not made by human beings) such as a mountain range or river that marks the border or limit of an area. The Alps, the Pyrenees, and the Rhine River are natural boundaries of France. See BOUNDARY.

**natural resources**: (NACH-uhr-ul REE-sohr-sez) **n.** Forms of wealth that come from nature, including oil, water, and metals like gold and silver. The United States is a country with many natural resources such as gold.

**United States Gold Coins - 1776**

**north**: (nohrth) **n.** A direction indicating the area toward the North Pole. The area at the top of a map is usually north.

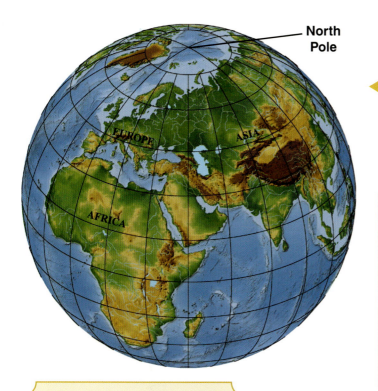

North Pole

**North Pole**: (NOHRTH POHL) **n.** The area at the top of the earth; the North Pole is 90° north of the equator. Explorers first reached the North Pole in 1909.

 **FUN FACTS**

Who got there first? In April 1909, Admiral Robert E. Peary reached the North Pole. However, just a week before he returned to civilization, another explorer, Frederick Cook, claimed that he had reached the Pole in April of 1908! After an investigation, Admiral Peary was given the credit.

**oasis**: (oh-AY-sis) **n.** A place in a desert that has water and where plants can grow. Thirsty travelers are happy to come upon an oasis in the desert.

**ocean**: (OH-shun) *n.* A very large body of water. To help us find our way around the world, we have "divided" the water separating the continents into four oceans—the Pacific, the Atlantic, the Indian, and the Arctic. The United States is bordered by the Pacific Ocean on the west and the Atlantic Ocean on the east.

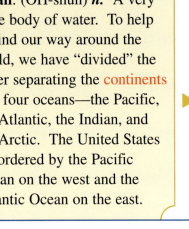

 **FUN FACTS**

Did you know that the Pacific Ocean is the largest ocean in the world? It covers about 64 million square miles. That's larger than all of the land in the world put together!

**ocean currents**: (OH-shun KUR-untz) *n.* Large amounts of water that move within or between oceans; generally, ocean currents flow clockwise in the Northern Hemisphere and counter clockwise in the Southern Hemisphere. Along the equator, ocean currents flow westward. Early European explorers followed ocean currents as they sailed toward the Americas. See TRADE WINDS.

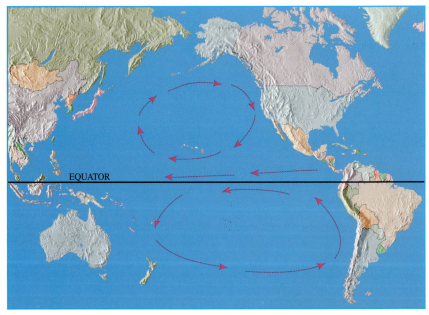

EQUATOR

**peninsula**: (puh-NIN-suh-luh) *n.* A piece of land surrounded by water on three sides. There are many peninsulas in Europe, including the Scandinavian, the Iberian, and the Italian peninsulas.

ATLANTIC OCEAN

Scandinavian Peninsula

EUROPE

Iberian Peninsula

Italian Peninsula

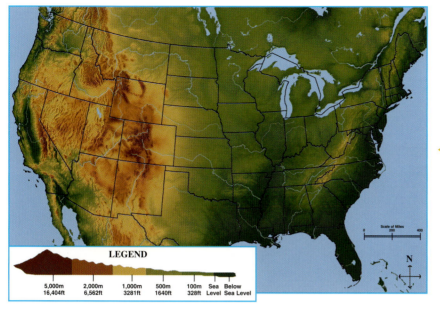

**physical map** (FIZ-uh-kul MAP) *n.* A map that shows the natural features of the earth's surface. There are two kinds of physical maps—relief maps and topographic maps. This physical map is a relief map of the United States.

**piedmont**: (PEED-mahnt) *n.* The area at the bottom of a mountain or highlands area. The Inca empire developed in the Andes region, which includes mountains and piedmont regions.

piedmont

Inca Empire - c. early 1500s

SOUTH AMERICA

**plain**: (playn) *n.* A large piece of flat land. Most people in the world live on plains.

"In geography one must think about the size of the entire earth, as well as its shape, and its position under the heavens …"

—Ptolemy, c. A.D. 150

**planet**: (PLAN-ut) *n.* A large sphere (ball) in the sky that moves around a star in an elliptical pattern. In our solar system, the earth is the third planet from the sun.

**plateau**: (pla-TOH) *n.* A large area of high, flat land. America's Desert Southwest includes many plateaus. You can see many plateaus in this photograph of the Grand Canyon. See MESA.

**political map**: (puh-LIT-i-kul MAP) *n.* A map that shows boundaries of states, countries, cities, and towns. This political map shows the United States of America.

**population**: (pahp-yoo-LAY-shun) *n.* All the people in a region, such as a country, city, or town. Every 10 years, we count the population of the United States to find out how many people live in the country.

 FUN FACTS

There are more than 6 billion people in the world today. Did you know that the population of the world increases by three people every second?

**population map**: (pahp-yoo-LAY-shun MAP) *n.* A map that shows the number of people living in a certain area. This population map shows the number of people who lived in America in 1910.

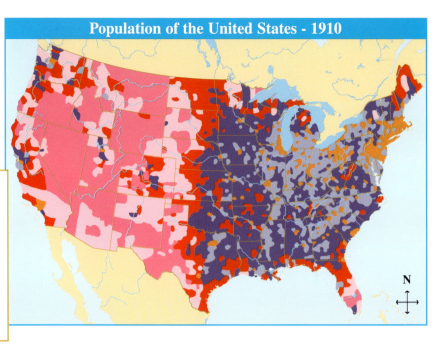

**Population of the United States - 1910**

**People per square mile**

Less than 5
5-15
15-45
45-120
120-225
More than 225

N

**port**: (pohrt) *n.* A place on a waterway for ships to load or unload cargo. Ports often give ships and boats protection from storms and rough water. See HARBOR.

WESTERN
HEMISPHERE

EASTERN
HEMISPHERE

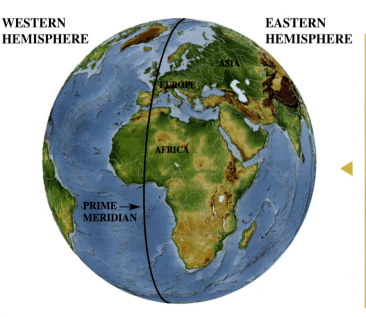

ASIA
EUROPE
AFRICA
PRIME → MERIDIAN

**prime meridian**: (PRIYM muh-RID-ee-un) *n.* An imaginary line that begins at the North Pole and goes through Greenwich, England to the South Pole. The prime meridian divides the earth in half. The land to the west of the prime meridian is in the Western Hemisphere and the land to the east of it is in the Eastern Hemisphere. The prime meridian is at 0 degrees longitude. See LONGITUDE.

**rain forest**: (RAYN FOHR-ist) *n.* An evergreen forest in a tropical region that receives at least 100 inches of rain per year. The soil is usually thin and poor, but the vegetation is rich and thick. Some Maya kingdoms developed in the rain forests of Central America.

**rapid**: (RAP-id) *n.* A part of a river where the water moves swiftly. Rapids are usually caused by a narrowing of the river bed. During the early 1800s, American factory owners in the Northeast took advantage of rapids as a source of power for their machines. See CATARACT and WATERFALL.

**ravine**: (ruh-VEEN) *n.* A small, narrow valley with steep sides. A ravine is larger than a gully and smaller than a canyon. Ravines are usually made by running water. See GAP, GORGE, and MOUNTAIN PASS.

**region**: (REE-jun) *n.* An area or place; a specific part of the world. The region we call the American Southwest is made up of the states of Arizona, New Mexico, Oklahoma, and Texas.

**The American Southwest**

Arizona

New Mexico

Oklahoma

Texas

N

**relief map**: (ri-LEEF MAP) *n.* A map that uses colors and shading to show the natural features (such as hills and valleys) of the earth. A relief map is one kind of physical map. This is a relief map of South America.

**South America**

N

LEGEND

| 5,000m 16,404ft | 3,000m 9,842ft | 2,000m 6,562ft | 1,000m 3281ft | 500m 1640ft | 100m 328ft | Sea Level | Below Sea Level |

**rice paddy**: (RIYS PAD-ee) *n.* A specially irrigated or flooded field where rice is grown. Rice paddies are very common in Asia.

 **FUN FACTS**

Wet-rice farming is common in Asia. Most rice farmers still use the same methods that were used 2,000 years ago. They break up the soil by hand with tools such as hoes and spades. Sometimes, they use a plow pulled by water buffalo, horses, or oxen.

# ⊕ *Voices in Geography* ⊕

"Nature has been for me, as long as I remember, a source of solace, inspiration, adventure, and delight …"

—Lorraine Anderson, 1988

**river**: (RIV-ur) *n.* A large, natural stream of water that empties into an ocean, lake, sea, or other body of water. Rivers provide water for many different animals, including human beings.

## ▼ FUN FACTS ▼

The United States has more than 10,000 miles of rivers.

### West Africa - Niger River Basin

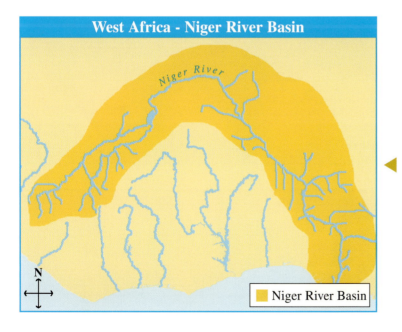

Niger River

N

■ Niger River Basin

**river basin**: (RIV-ur BAY-sun) *n.* An area of land that contains a river and all the streams that flow into it. By the late 1400s, the Songhai of West Africa created an empire that dominated the Niger River Basin.

"[The savannah has] grass which rises to heights of 12 feet overhead and shuts in the narrow trails … with here and there a few low trees all but hidden from view."

—Preston E. James, 1930

**Sahel**: (suh-HEEL) *n.* The flat, dry grasslands in western Africa between the Sahara desert on the north and the tropical forest areas on the south; this treeless area gets about 4-8 inches of rain a year. This photo shows camels in the Sahel region.

**savannah**: (suh-VAN-uh) *n.* An area of flat, treeless grasslands in tropical regions. Some of Africa's great civilizations developed in the savannah region.

N

S A H A R A

SAHEL

SAVANNAH

Least vegetation

Most vegetation

**scale**: (skayl) *n.* A line on a map that shows how the distance between places on a map compares with the real distance between the same places. One part of the scale on this map equals 100 miles.

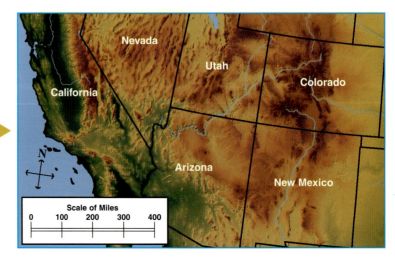

Nevada

Utah

California

Colorado

Arizona

New Mexico

N

Scale of Miles

0    100    200    300    400

## 🌏 *Voices in Geography* 🌏

"Alone, alone, all, all, alone; alone on a wide, wide sea."

—Samuel Taylor Coleridge, 1798

**The Mediterranean Sea**

EUROPE

*Mediterranean Sea*

AFRICA

N

**sea**: (see) *n.* A large body of water, usually salt water, that is either within an ocean or surrounded by land. The ancient Romans created an empire around the Mediterranean Sea.

**sea level**: (SEE LEV-ul) *n.* The level of the surface of the ocean. At 282 feet below sea level, Death Valley in California is the lowest spot in the Americas. See DEPTH.

 **FUN FACTS**

The Dead Sea is called "dead" because fish and other sea creatures cannot live in it. They cannot live in the water because it is so salty. The water of the Dead Sea is five times saltier than most sea water.

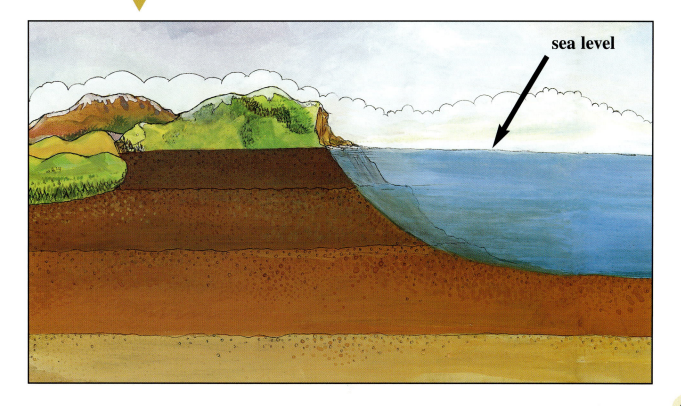

sea level

# Voices in Geography

"The voyage of discovery lies not in seeking new horizons, but in seeing with new eyes."

—Marcel Proust (1871-1922)

**shore**: (shohr) *n.* The land bordering a large body of water. Colonists from Europe landed on the shores of North America in the early 1600s. See COAST.

**south**: (sowth) *n.* A direction indicating the area toward the South Pole. The area at the bottom of a map is usually south.

**S**

**South Pole**: (SOWTH POHL) *n.* The area at the bottom of the earth; the South Pole is 90° south of the equator. Explorers first reached the South Pole in 1911.

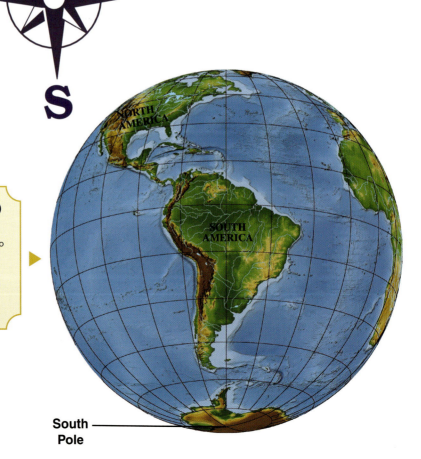

South Pole

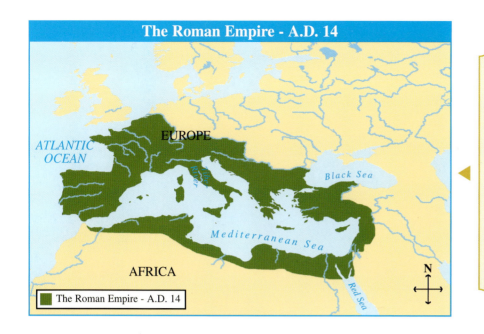

**The Roman Empire - A.D. 14**

ATLANTIC OCEAN

EUROPE

Black Sea

Mediterranean Sea

AFRICA

Red Sea

N

■ The Roman Empire - A.D. 14

**special purpose map**: (SPESH-ul PUR-pus MAP) *n.* A drawing of an area or region that shows special information such as weather, population, or historical boundaries. Picture symbols are often used on special purpose maps. This special purpose map shows the size of the Roman Empire in A.D. 14.

**steppe**: (step) *n.* A plain with few or no trees. From early times, groups of nomads have lived in the steppe region of northern China.

PORTUGAL

SPAIN

ATLANTIC OCEAN

Mediterranean Sea

AFRICA

N

**strait**: (strayt) *n.* A narrow passage of water joining two larger bodies of water. The Strait of Gibraltar connects the Atlantic Ocean and the Mediterranean Sea. See CHANNEL.

**stratified site**: (STRAT-uh-fiyd SIYT) *n.* A place where archaeologists dig into the earth to expose layers of materials. This is a stratified site in Africa where Mary and Louis Leakey found fossils of prehistoric peoples.

**street map**: (STREET MAP) *n.* A map that shows streets and such things as rivers and parks. A street map is handy to have in order to find your way around a city or town.

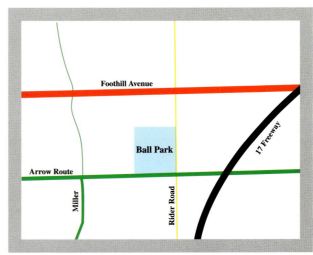

**subcontinent**: (suhb-KAHN-tuh-nent) *n.* A large piece of land, somewhat separated but still a part of a continent. India is a subcontinent of Asia.

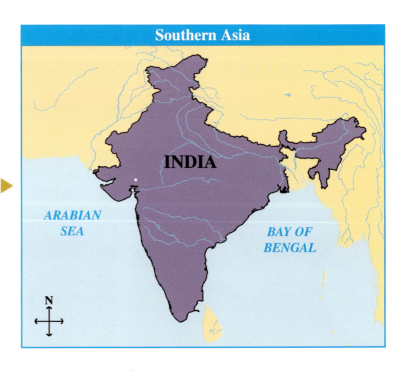

## Boundaries of the Tectonic Plates

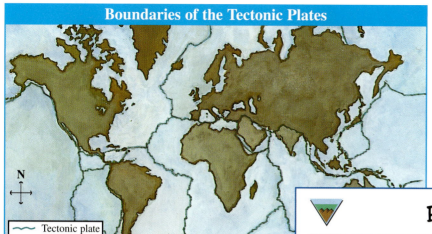

N

Tectonic plate boundaries

**tectonic plate**: (tek-TAHN-ik PLAYT) *n.* A large piece of the earth's crust. Tectonic plates that bump into each other cause earthquakes.

## FUN FACTS

Millions of years ago, the land of the earth formed one supercontinent, Pangea. Over time, Pangea broke apart into separate tectonic plates. Tectonic plates are always moving slowly in different directions. (They move from 1 inch to 6 inches per year—about how fast your fingernails grow!)

PANGEA

**terrace**: (TER-is) *n.* A flat, narrow piece of ground cut into a steep slope; usually to create flat land for farming. Farmers cut terraces into hillsides to create more farm land.

**terrain**: (tuh-RAYN) *n.* The natural features of land, such as hills, valleys, plains, or mountains. As early settlers moved westward, they traveled over different kinds of terrain, including high mountains.

47

**topographic map**: (tahp-oh-GRAF-ik MAP) *n.* A map that uses lines to show the elevation of natural features (such as hills and valleys) of the earth. A topographic map is one kind of physical map. This topographic map illustrates a way to show elevation.

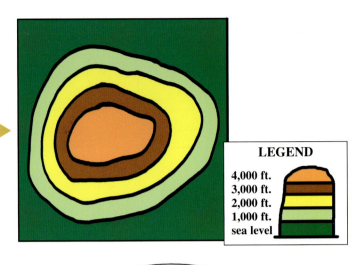

LEGEND

4,000 ft.
3,000 ft.
2,000 ft.
1,000 ft.
sea level

**trade winds**: (TRAYD WINDZ) *n.* A system of winds that always blows in the same direction; in the Northern Hemisphere, the trade winds (called the "northeast trade winds") blow from the northeast; in the Southern Hemisphere, the trade winds (called the "southeast trade winds") blow from the southeast. Since early times, sailors have relied on the trade winds to help them sail quickly across the ocean. See OCEAN CURRENTS.

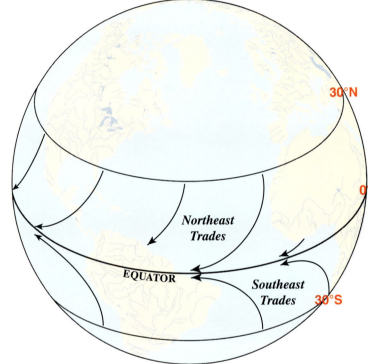

30°N

0°

Northeast Trades

EQUATOR

Southeast Trades

30°S

**tributary**: (TRIB-yoo-ter-ee) *n.* A small river (or stream) that flows into a larger river. From this picture you can see a river and one of its tributaries.

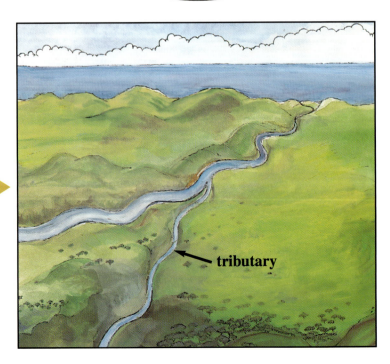

tributary

# 🌎 *Voices in Geography* 🌎

"… the best map to aid the geographer in forecasting settlement in a new country is one of the natural vegetation."

—Griffith Taylor, 1937

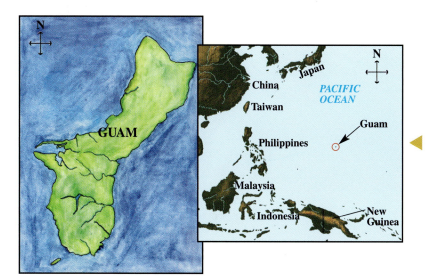

**United States territory**: (yoo-NIYT-id STAYTS TER-i-tohr-ee) *n.* A part of the United States that has a governor and its own legislature (law-making group), but is not a state. Guam is a United States territory.

**valley**: (VAL-ee) *n.* Low land between hills or mountains. It is usually warmer in valleys because the hills or mountains block the winds. See RAVINE and GORGE.

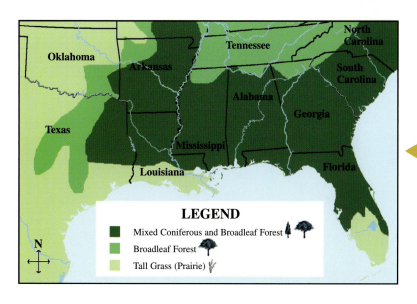

**vegetation map**: (vej-i-TAY-shun MAP) *n.* A map that shows plant life such as forest, woodland, scrub, grassland, and desert. This vegetation map shows the kinds of trees and grassland found in the southeastern United States.

**volcano**: (vahl-KAY-noh) *n.* A hole in the earth's crust through which hot ashes or lava (melted rock) come out. The Hawaiian Islands were formed by volcanoes.

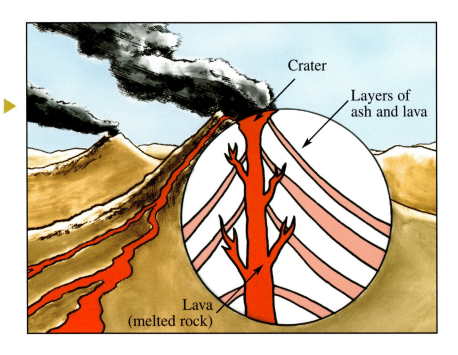

Crater

Layers of ash and lava

Lava (melted rock)

**waterfall**: (WAHT-uhr-fawl) *n.* A steep fall of water from a stream or river. In the 1800s, American factory owners in the Northeast took advantage of waterfalls as a source of power for their machines. See CATARACT and RAPIDS.

 FUN FACTS

The tallest waterfall in the world is Angel Falls in Venezuela. It is 3,212 feet high. Do you know how long it takes for the water to drop? Count slowly from 1 to 14. That's about how long it takes for water at the top of the waterfall to reach the bottom!

**weather**: (WETH-ur) *n.* The day-to-day changes in temperature and rainfall. Weather has an important influence on people's lives. See CLIMATE.

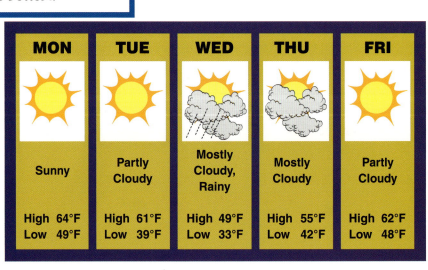

| MON | TUE | WED | THU | FRI |
|---|---|---|---|---|
| Sunny | Partly Cloudy | Mostly Cloudy, Rainy | Mostly Cloudy | Partly Cloudy |
| High 64°F | High 61°F | High 49°F | High 55°F | High 62°F |
| Low 49°F | Low 39°F | Low 33°F | Low 42°F | Low 48°F |

# Appendix I: Geographical Features and Terms in Spanish

Visit www.ballard-tighe.com to find translations of the features and terms in other languages.

**agriculture, industry, and resources map**: agricultura, industria y mapa de recursos
**aqueduct**: acueducto
**archipelago**: archipiélago
**atlas**: guía de carreteras y mapas, atlas
**bay**: angra, bahía
**boundary**: límite, línea limítrofe
**canal**: canal
**canyon**: cañón
**cape**: cabo
**cataract**: catarata
**cave**: cueva, caverna
**channel**: canal
**city**: ciudad
**cliff**: risco, acantilado
**climate**: clima
**coast**: costa
**commercial harbor**: puerto comercial
**compass rose**: rosa de los vientos
**continent**: continente
**Continental Divide**: División Continental
**dam**: embalse, represa
**degree**: grado
**delta**: delta
**demographic change**: cambio demográfico
**depth**: profundidad
**desert**: desierto
**earthquake**: terremoto
**elevation**: elevación, altitud
**environmental pollution**: contaminación ambiental
**equator**: ecuador, línea ecuatorial
**erosion**: erosión
**Fertile Crescent**: El Valle del Tigris y Eufrates
**flood plain**: área de inundación
**foothill**: estribaciones
**forest**: selva, bosque
**frontier**: frontera
**gap**: hondanada
**gazetteer**: diccionario geográfico
**geographer**: geógrafo
**geography**: geografía
**glacier**: glaciar

**globe**: globo, mapamundo
**gorge**: cañón, barranco
**Great Lakes**: Grandes Lagos
**gulf**: golfo
**harbor**: puerto
**hemisphere**: hemisferio
**hill**: cerro, loma
**inlet**: acceso, ensenada
**international date line**: línea de cambio de fecha
**irrigation systems**: sistema de irrigación
**island**: isla
**isle**: isla
**isthmus**: istmo
**lake**: lago
**land bridge**: puente
**landmark**: hito, mojón, señal
**landmass**: gran extensión
**latitude**: latitud
**legend**: epígrafe
**loess highlands**: montaña fertilizada por el viento
**longitude**: longitud
**map**: mapa
**marsh**: pantano
**mesa**: meseta
**mountain**: montaña, monte
**mountain pass**: paso montañoso
**mountain range**: cordillera, montañas
**natural boundary**: límite natural
**natural resources**: recursos naturales
**north**: norte
**North Pole**: Polo Norte
**oasis**: oasis
**ocean**: océano
**ocean currents**: corrientes oceánicas
**peninsula**: península
**physical map**: mapa físico
**piedmont**: tierras bajas
**plain**: llano, campo
**planet**: planeta
**plateau**: altiplano
**political map**: mapa político
**population**: población

**population map**: mapa de población
**port**: puerto
**prime meridian**: meridiano de Greenwich
**rain forest**: bosque húmedo, bosque lluvioso
**rapid**: rápidos
**ravine**: barranco
**region**: región
**relief map**: mapa de relieve
**rice paddy**: cultivo de arroz, arrozal
**river**: río
**river basin**: cuenca del río, lecho fluvial
**Sahel**: Sahara árido
**savannah**: sabana, llano
**scale**: escala
**sea**: mar
**sea level**: nivel del mar
**shore**: orilla, playa
**south**: sur
**South Pole**: Polo Sur
**special purpose map**: mapa especializado
**steppe**: estepa
**strait**: estrecho
**stratified site**: área de cultivo
**street map**: mapa de carreteras o rutas
**subcontinent**: subcontinente
**tectonic plate**: placa tectónica
**terrace**: terraza, hilera
**terrain**: topografía del terreno
**topographic map**: mapa de topografía, mapa topográfico
**trade winds**: vientos alisios, vientos generales
**tributary**: afluente, tributario
**United States territory**: territorio de Estados Unidos (de América)
**valley**: cuenca, valle
**vegetation map**: mapa de vegetación
**volcano**: volcán
**waterfall**: cascada, catarata
**weather**: tiempo, clima

# Appendix II: Political Map of the United States

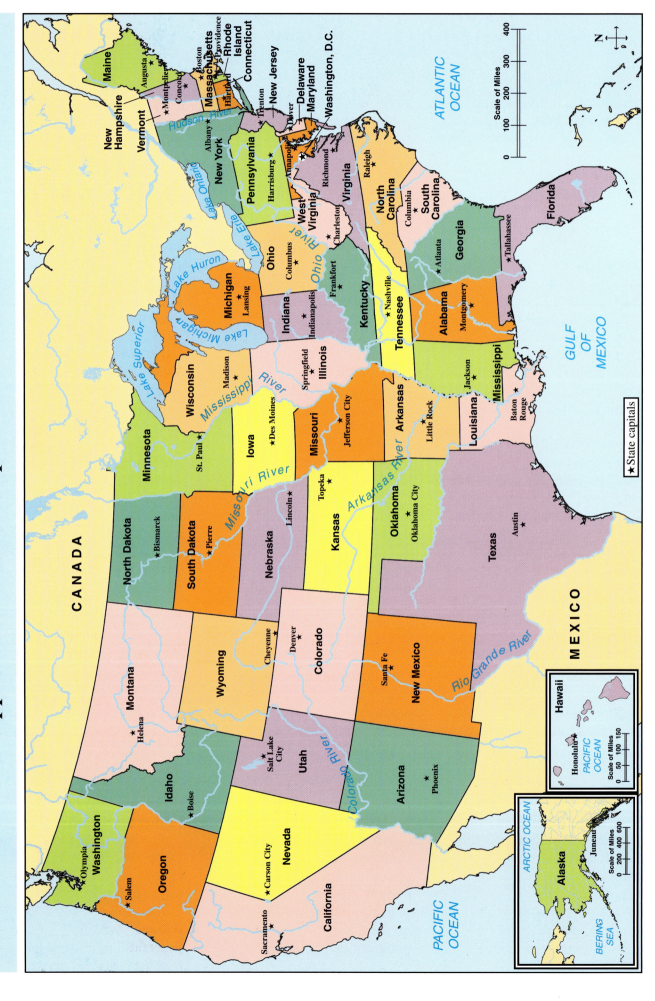

# Appendix III: Relief Map of the United States

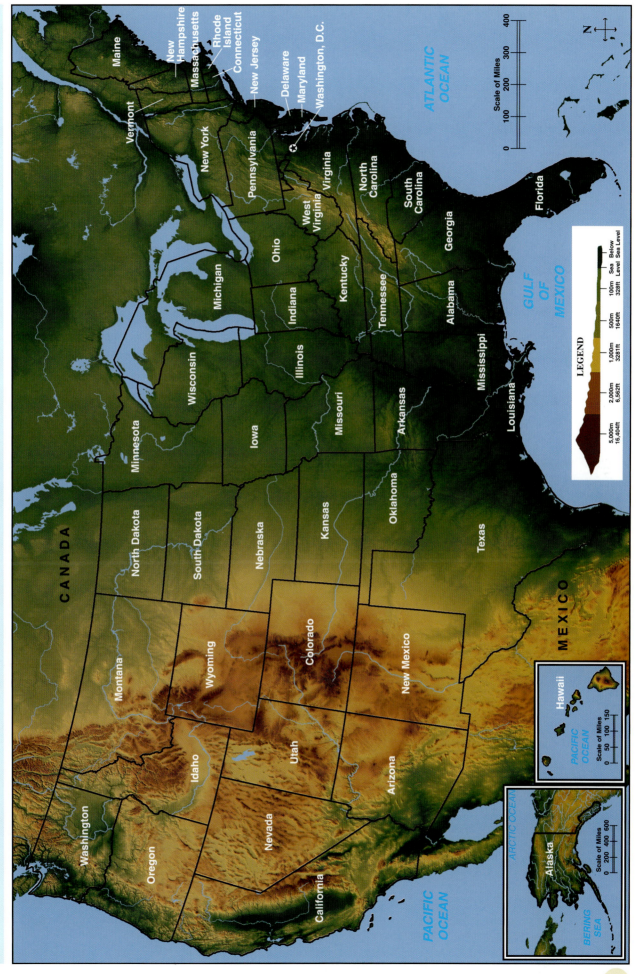

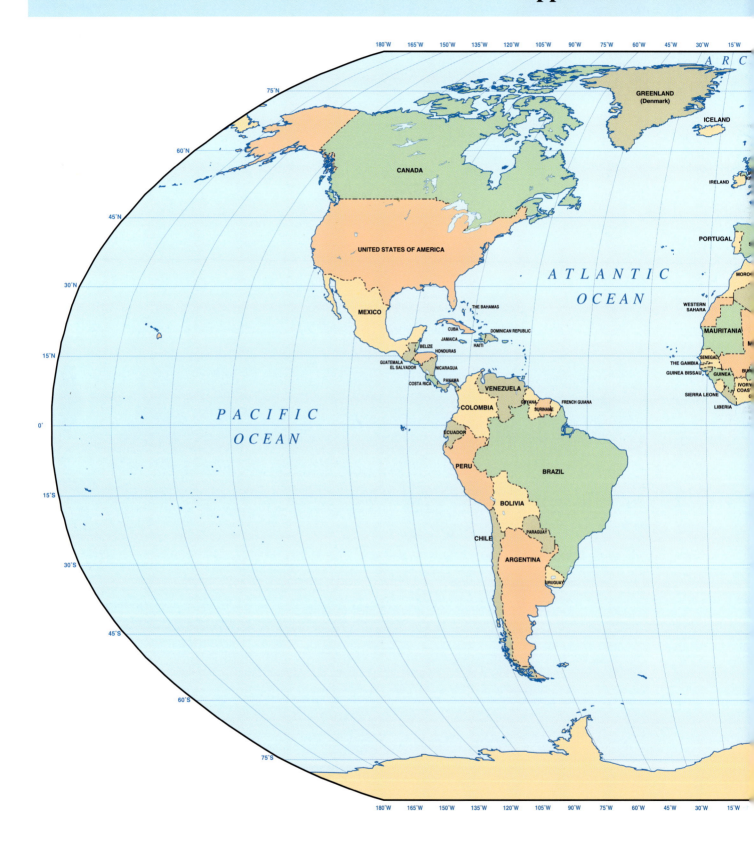

Sources for Political Labels: The Central Intelligence Agency's *The World Fact Book* and Office of the Geographer and Global Issues, Bureau of Intelligence and Research, U.S. Department of State, Washington, D.C.

# Map of the World

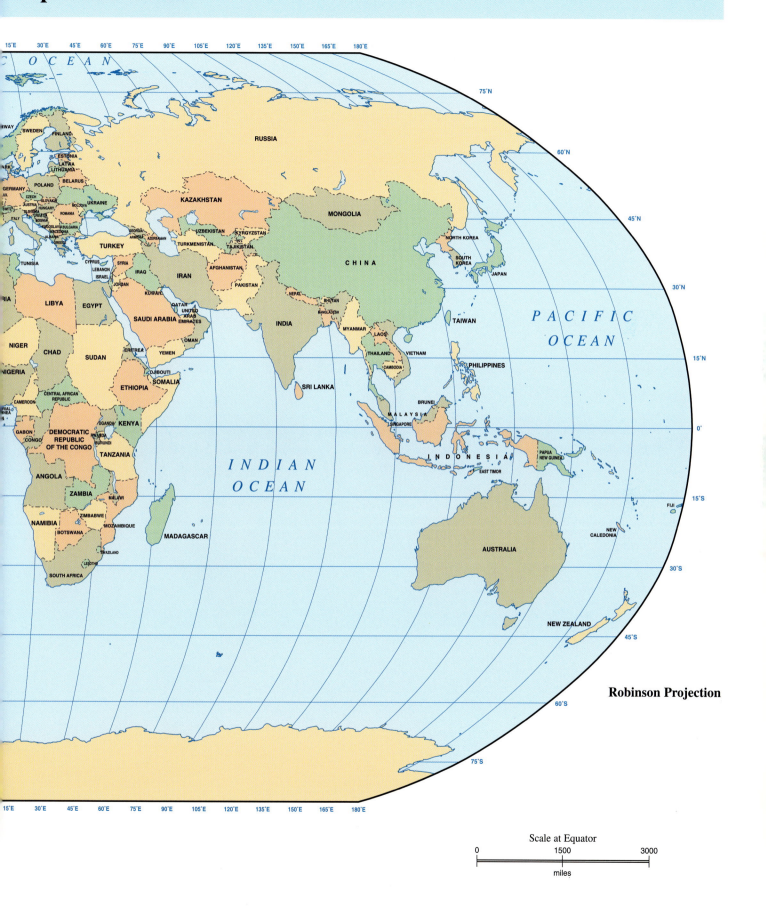

**Robinson Projection**

Scale at Equator

0    1500    3000

miles

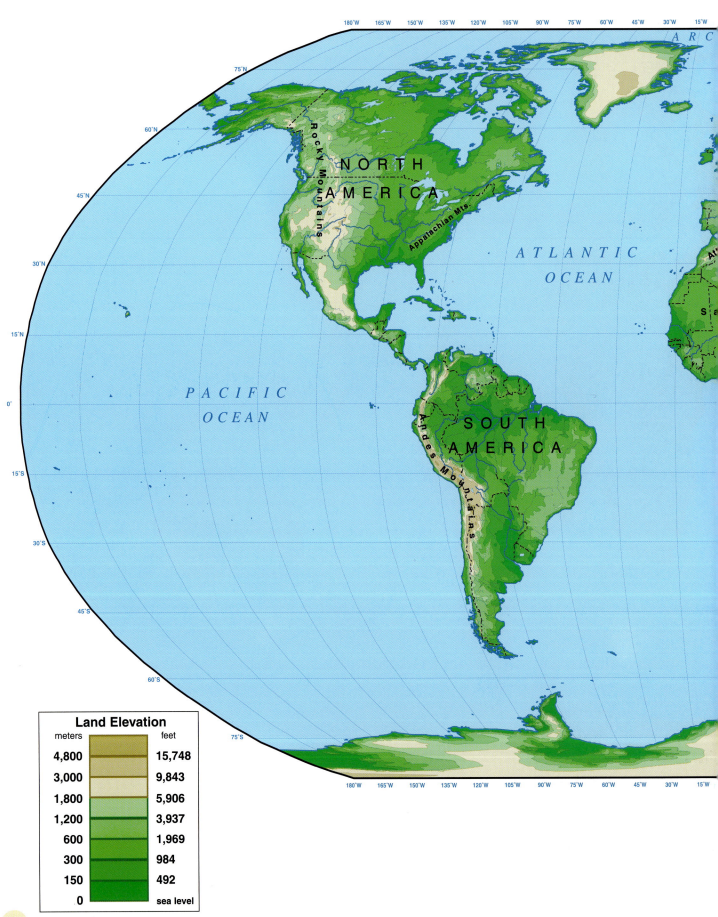

**Land Elevation**

| meters | | feet |
|---|---|---|
| 4,800 | | 15,748 |
| 3,000 | | 9,843 |
| 1,800 | | 5,906 |
| 1,200 | | 3,937 |
| 600 | | 1,969 |
| 300 | | 984 |
| 150 | | 492 |
| 0 | | sea level |

# Map of the World

**Robinson Projection**

Scale at Equator

0    1500    3000

miles

# Appendix VI: World Statistics

| Longest Rivers | Length in miles | Oceans and Major Seas | Area in square miles |
|---|---|---|---|
| Nile, Africa | 4,145 | Pacific Ocean | 63,855,000 |
| Amazon, South America | 4,007 | Atlantic Ocean | 31,744,000 |
| Mississippi-Missouri-Red Rock, U.S.A. | 3,710 | Indian Ocean | 28,417,000 |
| Chang Jiang (Yangtze), China | 3,500 | Arctic Ocean | 5,427,000 |
| Ob'-Irtysh, Russia-Kazakhstan | 3,362 | Caribbean Sea | 970,000 |
| Yenisey-Angara, Asia | 3,100 | Mediterranean Sea | 969,000 |
| Huang He (Yellow), China | 2,950 | South China Sea | 895,000 |

| Highest Mountains | Height in feet | Major Lakes | Area in square miles |
|---|---|---|---|
| Everest, Nepal-China | 29,028 | Caspian Sea, Asia | 143,243 |
| K2 (Godwin Austen), Pakistan-China | 28,250 | Lake Superior, U.S.A.-Canada | 31,820 |
| Kanchenjunga, Nepal-India | 28,208 | Lake Victoria, Africa | 26,628 |
| Lhotse, Nepal-China | 27,923 | Lake Huron, U.S.A.-Canada | 23,010 |
| Makalu, Nepal-China | 27,789 | Lake Michigan, U.S.A. | 22,400 |
| Dhaulagiri, Nepal | 26,810 | Aral Sea, Kazakhstan-Uzbekistan | 15,830 |
| Nanga Parbat, Pakistan | 26,660 | Lake Tanganyika, Africa | 12,650 |

Source: *New Century World Atlas*, 2000

# Appendix VII: Vowel Pronunciation Key

This pronunciation key shows how to pronounce the vowels, which are the most problematic sounds in English pronunciation.

| SYMBOL | KEY WORDS |
|---|---|
| a | ant, man |
| ay | cake, May |
| ah | clock, arm |
| aw | salt, ball |
| e | neck, hair |
| ee | ear, key |
| i | chick, skin |
| iy | five, tiger |
| oh | coat, soda |
| oi | boy, coin |
| ohr | board, door |
| oo | blue, boot |
| ow | cow, owl |
| u | foot, wolf, bird, and the schwa sound used in final syllables followed by 'l,' 'r,' 's,' 'm,' 't,' or 'n,' for example, children (CHIL-<u>drun</u>) |
| uh | bug, uncle, and other schwa sounds, such as, kangaroo (kang-<u>guh</u>-ROO) |

Source:  The vowel pronunciation key is derived from the *American Heritage Dictionary of the English Language*, 1981; *Oxford American Dictionary: Heald Colleges Edition*, 1982; *Webster's New World College Dictionary, Third Edition*, 1990.  Please note surrounding letters may affect the vowel sound slightly.

With the *Explore Geography Picture Dictionary*, you and your students are on your way to uncovering the wonders of geography. Why teach geography along with history? Historical events are inextricably tied to the physical location and resources in a place. Imagine studying ancient Egypt without understanding the role of the Nile River in the development of the Egyptian civilization. The *Explore Geography Picture Dictionary* provides a foundation of basic geographical facts to help students become familiar with the themes and standards set forth by the Joint Committee on Geographic Education of the National Council for Geographic Education and the Association of American Geographers. This will help them better understand the world and history.

Each dictionary entry contains a **pronunciation guide**, a **definition**, a **sample sentence**, and a **picture**. To help students learn how to pronounce the words, we have created a simplified, phonetic pronunciation for each entry. To introduce students to the dictionary, review with them the information on page 4 as well as the pronunciation key on page 58.

You can find Spanish translations of the geographical terms in Appendix I. We also offer translations in other languages online, including Arabic, Hmong, and Korean. To find these translations, go to **www.ballard-tighe.com** and enter the key words **"geography dictionary"** in the **"Find a Product"** area. On the right side of the *Explore Geography Picture Dictionary* page, select **"Online Materials"** from the product menu.

The *Explore Geography Picture Dictionary* can be used with any social studies curriculum. It also can be used as a springboard for geography-based games and activities. Here are some fun activities:

- **Find the Term—FAST!** Ask students to find examples of geographic terms. Have them note their start/stop times. The goal is to beat their own times.

- **What's the Connection?** Have students choose an entry with a link to another entry, and then explain the connection. For example, the entry for dam says, "See irrigation systems." The connection? A dam is a kind of irrigation system.

- **Downloadable Geography Activities.** Have students complete activity sheets to practice various skills. You can access the activity sheets and directions to use them by going to **www.ballard-tighe.com** and entering the key words **"geography dictionary"** in the **"Find a Product"** area. On the right side of the *Explore Geography Picture Dictionary* page, select **"Online Materials"** from the product menu.

Have fun as you EXPLORE geography with your students!

*Roberta Stathis*          *Leila Langston*          *Cari Dunkin*

# Index

The definition of the word is found on the page printed in red.